BESTIE

STEVE BEST

INDEX

First published 1996 by Boxtree Limited in association with Paperlink Limited, 356 Kennington Road, London SE11 4LD

This edition published 2002 for Index Books Limited by Boxtree
an imprint of Pan Macmillan Ltd
Pan Macmillan, 20 New Wharf Road, London N1 9RR
Basingstoke and Oxford
Associated companies throughout the world
www.panmacmillan.com

ISBN 0 7522 1130 7

9 8 7 6 5 4 3 2 1

A CIP catalogue record for this book is available from the British Library.

Printed by Mackays of Chatham

DESPITE WINNING THE LOTTERY, THEY STILL
REMEMBERED THEIR OLD FRIENDS

UNFORTUNATELY FOR THE ROAD BUILDERS, IT
WAS THE DAY THE TEDDY BEARS HAD THEIR PICNIC

WHAT HE LOVED MOST ABOUT HER
WAS HER SENSE OF HUMOUR.

THE GERMANS HADN'T COME OUT OF THEIR
JUMP FORMATION QUITE AS PLANNED.

ELVIS OFTEN WISHED HE WAS IN HELL WITH
ALL THE OTHER ROCK 'N ROLL MUSICIANS

SHE FOUND IT HARD TO DENY THE
CHARGE OF SEXUAL HARASSMENT

THE EFFECTS OF A LONG COACH TOURING
HOLIDAY WERE BEGINNING TO SHOW.

THE CHESHIRE CAT EXPLAINED TO ALICE
THAT HE WAS A GREAT ADMIRER OF TONY BLAIR

THE CATALOGUE HAD PROMISED THAT THE
SPECIALLY DESIGNED T-SHIRT WOULD MAKE
HIM LOOK LIKE A SEX MACHINE.

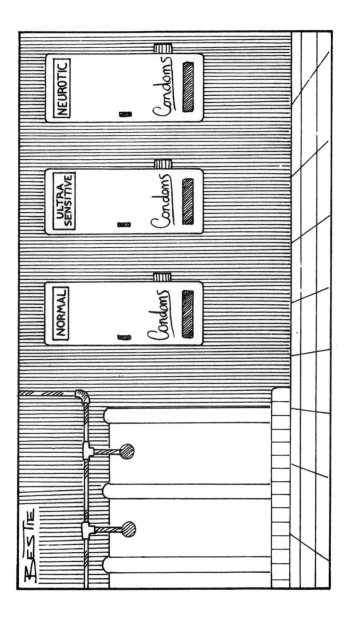

ONCE HE TRIED A NEW FITNESS TECHNIQUE
HIS BEER-BELLY PROBLEM WAS SOON BEHIND HIM

"WHAT MAKES YOU SO SURE THAT I'M A LEO?"

"I THINK I'VE WORKED OUT WHERE THAT SNIPER'S HIDING"

"CANNIBALS! THANK GOD FOR THAT FRIDAY.
~ I THOUGHT THEY WERE 18-30 HOLIDAY MAKERS.

IT WAS OBVIOUS TO DOROTHY
THAT SCARECROW NEEDED A BRAIN

THE NIGHT OF 'THE SUN'S' THEATRE CRITIC.

ROYAL DIVORCES HAVE ALWAYS BEEN
PAINFUL, MESSY AFFAIRS

BESTIE

GENTS

AFTER A FEW PINTS, HE HAD A
RATHER SURREAL DREAM

WHILE ANSWERING A QUESTION ON SURREALISM HIS PEN RAN OUT.

"It says.....NOW GET OUT OF THAT, SUCKERS!"

MONA WAS TRYING NOT TO SMILE AS
SHE WAITED FOR HER SILENT FART
TO REACH LEONARDO.

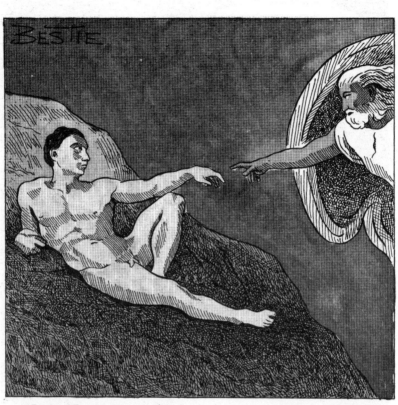

GOD SHOWED ADAM WHAT HE'D HAVE
TO USE UNTIL HE'D CREATED EVE.

SUPERMODELS HAVE ALWAYS BEEN OBSESSED
BY HOW TO KEEP THEIR SHAPE AND FITNESS

THEY WERE LATER CHARGED WITH IMITATING A CONSTABLE.

MANET MANAGED TO CAPTURE THE
EXPERIENCE OF PARISIAN BARS

LIFE BECAME DIFFICULT FOR VAN GOGH
AFTER HE CUT HIS EAR OFF.

"YOU'RE WASTING YOUR TIME,
MONET ONLY PAINTS THE LILIES."

"ADMIT IT, THIS IS YOUR
FIRST TIME ISN'T IT?"

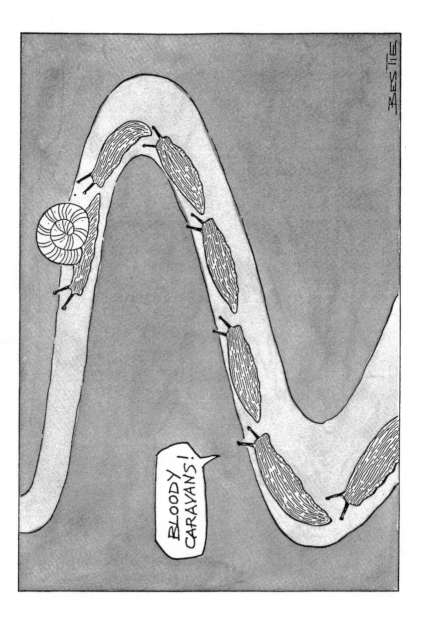

RUMOURS THAT THE TUNNEL WOULD BRING CLOSER LINKS WITH FRANCE, SENT PANIC ROUND THE VILLAGE POND.

SEABIRDS FREQUENTLY USE RHYMING SLANG

"THIS IS IT GEORGE, HEAVEN OR HELL!"

"PERSONALLY I WOULDN'T RECOMMEND SPAIN"

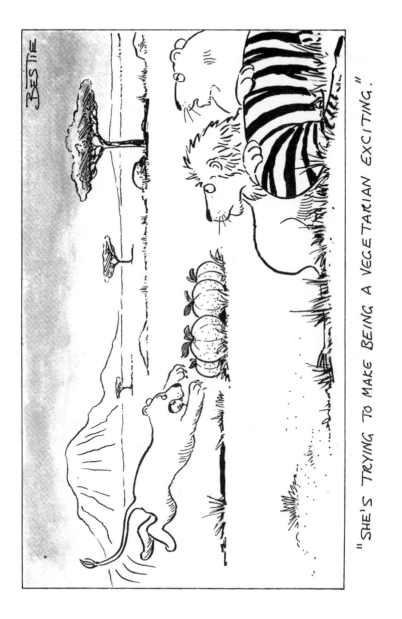

"SHE'S TRYING TO MAKE BEING A VEGETARIAN EXCITING."

CHAMELEONS FIND IT PARTICULARLY DIFFICULT TO DISGUISE THE FACT THAT THEY'VE BEEN DOWN THE PUB.

"DON'T EAT THE HARD BIT ON IT'S BACK, THEY MAKE YOU FART!"

"LOOKS LIKE JUST CHIPS AGAIN TONIGHT"

"IF YOU REALLY LOVED ME YOU'D
HAVE GIVEN ME FLOWERS"

HE WAS A ROMANTIC FOOL
BUT HE WASN'T STUPID.

HE WAS FINDING IT MORE AND MORE
DIFFICULT TO DISGUISE THE FACT THAT
HE HAD THE 'HOTS' FOR HER.

ALL LOVERS AT SOMETIME HAVE TO MAKE AN
IMPORTANT DECISION ～ DO THEY EAT THEIR
ROMANTIC SUPPER BEFORE OR AFTER MAKING LOVE

NOT KNOWING HOW TO TELL HIM, SHE HOPED
SUBTLE BODY LANGUAGE WOULD WORK

IT WAS VALENTINES DAY AND SHE WAS
DETERMINED THAT TONIGHT HE
WOULD MAKE LOVE LIKE A TIGER.

THE FIRST TIME THEY MADE LOVE WAS MAGIC

HE KNEW WHAT TO SAY TO TURN HER ON
AND SHE KNEW WHICH BUTTONS TO PRESS

SHE WAS OVERJOYED WHEN HE UTTERED THOSE THREE MAGICAL WORDS—'SOD THE FOOTBALL!'

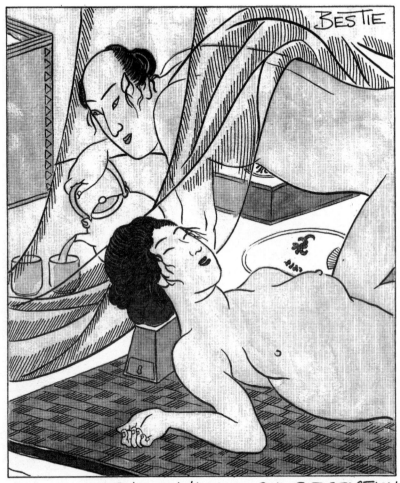

GOOD LOVERS KNOW HOW TO GIVE SATISFACTION
FIRST THING IN THE MORNING.

CYRANO DE BERGERAC COULDN'T DISGUISE HIS LOVE
FOR ROXANNE ANY LONGER

LUCKILY RUDOLPH VALENTINO'S FILMS WERE SILENT

BY THE 14TH RE-TAKE
BOGART WAS PISSED.

SERGEANT WARDEN WAS ABOUT TO LOSE
HIS JOB AS 'LOOK-OUT' AT PEARL HARBOUR.

SHE SUDDENLY REALISED WHY
DR. FRANKENSTEIN HAD CREATED HER.

SUDDENLY TERROR STRUCK
~ HE'D NEVER SEEN A NAKED WOMAN BEFORE

WHILE SINGING IN THE HILLS MARIA SUDDENLY
REALISED SHE DIDN'T WANT TO BE A NUN AFTER ALL

IT WAS HIGH NOON. THE STREET WAS DESERTED
~ EXCEPT OF COURSE FOR THE MAD DOG AND ENGLISHMAN

HE WASN'T SURE WHETHER TO SHOW HER HOW MUCH HE
WANTED HER, OR KEEP IT UNDER HIS HAT.

WENDY HAD BEEN TAUGHT NEVER TO TRUST BOYS AND TO ALWAYS TAKE HER OWN PRECAUTIONS.

LONG JOHN SILVER FIRST MET 'BLIND PUGH'
WHEN THEY WERE CABIN BOYS TOGETHER

LONG JOHN'S LONG JOHNS.

MAID MARION SUSPECTED ROBIN WASN'T QUITE
READY FOR AN EMOTIONAL INVOLVEMENT.

MAID MARION TOLD ROBIN SHE LOVED THE POOR BUT HAD DECIDED TO STAY WITH THE RICH.

"REMEMBER ICARUS DON'T FLY TOO CLOSE TO THE SUN ~ GO TO BRITAIN FOR YOUR HOLIDAY"

UNFORTUNATELY FOR JACK, THE GIANT
WAS A WELSH NATIONALIST.

LUCKILY THE GOOSE THAT LAID GOLDEN EGGS COULD AFFORD TO 'GO PRIVATE' FOR HAEMORRHOID TREATMENT

THE WOMEN OF LILLIPUT
WERE PARTICULARLY CURIOUS

DINOSAURS DIED OUT DURING THE PLATONIC PERIOD

HEDGEHOGS TRIED THEIR HARDEST
TO UN-INVENT THE WHEEL

THE ROMAN'S ROAD BUILDING SCHEME WAS GOING
TO PLAN UNTIL THEY DISCOVERED SCRUMPY.

HIS BROTHERS TRIED THEIR BEST
TO REASSURE HIM

THE 16TH CENTURY PRODUCED
OUR GREATEST WRITER
~ AND OUR WORST BARBER!

"JUST A KISS WILL DO HARDY!"

" EMILY! REFINED LADIES DO NOT REVEAL AN ANKLE IN PUBLIC "

BESTIE

A NEW MEMBER OF THE HITLER YOUTH WAS DETERMINED TO ENJOY HIS DAY OUT TO NUREMBERG.

TWO SINNERS MADE A DESPERATE
ATTEMPT TO GET ABOARD THE ARK

HIS HAIR WASN'T THE FIRST THING
THAT SAMSON CHECKED.

NOT ALL THE PHILISTINES WERE DESPONDENT
WHEN DAVID SLEW GOLIATH

"WHAT DO YOU MEAN 'IT'S A BIT MUDDY'?"

"I'M ONLY FISHING TODAY"

AT THE LAST SUPPER JESUS HAD A SHREWD IDEA WHO HAD BETRAYED HIM.

HE WAS ALMOST READY FOR THE
FAMILY CHRISTMAS GET-TOGETHER

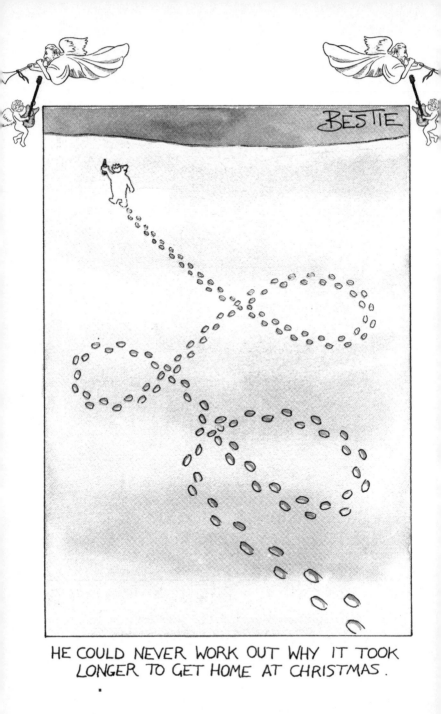

HE COULD NEVER WORK OUT WHY IT TOOK
LONGER TO GET HOME AT CHRISTMAS.

CINDERELLA AND PRINCE CHARMING
WEREN'T THE ONLY ONES WHO FELL
IN LOVE THIS CHRISTMAS

BABY JESUS ENJOYED PLAYING
WITH HIS NEW TORCH.